Pausing *in* HIS Presence

SHERI POWELL

SLP COMPANY
Sharing the Lord with People

Cover designed by Dave A. Humphrey Consulting
Book edited by Sherrie Clark www.SherrieClark.com
Back cover photo taken by Christina Johnson www.SoulProspers.com
Printed by: Quad Graphics www.QC.com
Published by SLP Company, P. O. Box 9172, Fleming Isle, FL 32006

Registered with the Library of Congress Case Number: 2014914587
ISBN: 978-0-692-27397-5

When you PAUSE, visit our website: www.PausingWithGod.com

You can contact the SLP Company or Sheri Powell at:
Email: PausingWithGod@gmail.com
Like us on Facebook: Facebook.com/PausingWithGod.com
Follow us on Twitter: @PausingWithHim

Or write us at:
SLP (Sharing the Lord with People) Company
C/O Sheri Powell
P. O. Box 9172
Fleming Isle, FL 32006

Printed in the United States of America
First Printing: 09/2014

DEDICATION

This book is dedicated to Addie Stevens. Words cannot express how instrumental you have been in my life. You are not only my aunt, but my spiritual mother. As one of your first pupils, I have learned how vital it is to pause in His Presence. You have and continue to train, teach, and mentor me to be a real woman of God.

You are a shut-in forerunner. I have witnessed your dedication and commitment in ushering God's daughters to wholeness. Many have been revived and refreshed as well as restored.

My prayer is that every daughter of Eve is blessed with a 'Titus woman' like you. We all need someone to walk with us, someone who unceasingly entreats the Lord on our behalf as we become who God has created us to be.

I thank God for you and I look forward to a greater spiritual manifestation of His presence in many lives in the days to come.

TABLE OF CONTENTS

FOREWORD

At whatever season in life this book finds you, your willingness to submit to prayer matters. On earth as in heaven, God has made the way possible for those who seek Him to experience the joy of intimacy with our Creator. Every person who calls on the Name of the Lord gets His attention.

Without letting this world gain our attention, we shall move nearer than ever to the things of the Spirit. This is not a time for distance from the Presence of God. This is a time of urgency ... a time for pausing to hear from God in your season of life. I am convinced; the unusually intimate pursuit of the truth will open new eyes and warm cold hearts. By God's grace and love, we shall discover fresh dimensions of the One who was set to transform our lives, even through the most challenging seasons of life.

Intimacy with God is His idea. He has taken the initiative, and prayer is His gift to us. Prayer is our response to the One who has called out to us and desires to be in a relationship with us.

Sheri Powell is an encourager. Let Sheri encourage you through God's Word to *PAUSE* and personally respond to God's invitation to deeper intimacy with Him.

Pastor Garry Wiggins
Evangel Temple Church
Jacksonville, Florida

ACKNOWLEDGEMENTS

A Mis Cinco Hijos, (To My Five Children),
What God has put together, no man can divide. Many do not know our story, but they'll get a glimpse of it in Fall of 2017, *There Are No Steps in This House*. We've had more than our share of tears, but we've also had limitless precious moments. I thank God for each of you and look forward to Him doing some great things in our family and in your individual lives. Amo a cada uno de ustedes con más que las palabras pueden decir. (I love each of you more than words can say.)

To Anthony (my beloved husband and friend),
I remember that day my cousin sang "Usher Me" at our wedding reception. The lyrics tell how a husband escorts his wife into the presence of the Lord. I was baffled by this selection. However as time passes, God continues to use you to do just that. May what God joined together continue to shed light on who He is and how He intended marriage to be. Thank you for giving me the freedom to be me. I love you with an everlasting love.

A mammoth thank you to my pastor, Garry Wiggins, my church family, my editor and my consulting team. To all my sister~friends who have tirelessly sat in His presence with me. To all those extra sets of eyes, you can pause; at least for a little while. I thank God for each of you, know that your patience, God-given talents and gifts supported in the birth of baby number two. May God continue to use us to be His salt and shine His light.

To My Heavenly Father,
It is hard to express a love that never ceases. I praise you for all that You have done, are doing and have promised to do. You are truly more than I'd ever imagined, You are my Healer, my Provider, my Shepherd, and my Friend.

INTRODUCTION

Genesis 2:21–23 (Life Application Bible) states, "Man gives life to woman; woman gives life to the world."

While women are looked upon to meet natural needs, her immense spiritual contribution must be noted. Women are created to be more than physical carriers. Women are born intercessors. There is nothing like a woman who knows how to pray in such a way that she and her prayers reach the throne of God.

A great case in point that exhibits the power behind intercession and women is found in the Book of Esther. She became an orphan at a young age and was raised by her cousin Mordecai.

One day when King Ahasuerus was drinking and being merry, he ordered Vashti, his queen, to appear before him and his guests. Vashti was beautiful but didn't think it was appropriate to be summoned in this fashion, so she refused to appear. In the midst of his anger, the king asked his wise men for advice on how to handle this matter.

One of them recommended that something had to be done immediately, before uproar started amongst the ladies. His advisors foresaw that Vashti's response and attitude would cause trouble in the kingdom. They suggested that it was in the king's best interest to remove Vashti.

Esther became part of the kingdom during the king's search for a replacement for Vashti. Though the king issued a decree that called beautiful young virgins to the palace, God strategically placed Esther in the province for such a time as this.

Though Esther was chosen to become the new bride to the King of Persia, she would also be the person who God would use to save a nation from being exterminated.

Esther has left us with an ageless example. In the midst of her predicament, she demonstrates the discipline as well as the secret of fasting and prayer. This deliberate entreaty of God still works today. As she went before the throne of God in heaven, she received what was necessary to go before the earthly king.

Like Esther in our times of fasting and praying, we are to be encouraged. We are not to focus on what we can see. Esther didn't shut in to get her way; she sought after God's face. With a willing heart and a listening ear, she waited for Him to order her steps.

As Esther emerged from this shut-in experience, her life and the lives of her people were never the same.

SHUT-IN TESTIMONIES

I knew that God had been calling me to draw closer to Him. There was so much going on in my life where I had sought His guidance, but did not find favor.

"Press in," is what He said when all else seemed to fail. "Not by strength or by power but by My spirit," said the Lord.

So when Sheri gave the invitation to the women's shut-in, I saw this as an opportunity to approach God in a different manner.

When Saul was to be anointed the first king of Israel, Samuel gave him instructions to travel toward home, and that on the way he would meet a company of prophet musicians. The prophets were to prophesy over him, and he would be "turned into a new man and given a new heart."

Praise God that we are given the gift of the Holy Spirit when we accept Christ as our Savior. We are made into a new man and given a new heart right away. But when we are distracted by the cares of the world, we may miss time for renewal and refreshment.

My mind and my spirit needed to be renewed. I desired to put my priorities in line with His. This shut-in that the Lord allowed me to attend was a wonderful time to do just this.

I experienced freedom with dance, prayer language, words of prophecy, and a freshness of the spirit; my heart was renewed.

Joanne Bracewell
Darien, Georgia

❖❖❖❖

Personal prayer time is imperative to our spiritual survival. But carving out time to rest in God's presence and waiting for His provision is equally essential.

My shut-in experience was like being sheathed within love. I was encased within the tangible, permeable love of Yeshua. My spirit heard His voice calling me to deny all mental disturbances. The Holy Spirit beckoned, lured, and wooed me into His presence.

Once I answered His call, I could literally feel Him subduing me.

This shut-in experience was beyond my intellectual capacity, for me it was an out-of-this-world encounter.

Jessica "Sunshine" Robinson
Jacksonville, Florida

❖❖❖❖

I praise God each time I reflect back on my shut-in experience. From the moment I arrived, I immediately felt welcomed. The presence of the Holy Spirit was prevalent.

I remember there was a vibe in the atmosphere. It was as if someone was waiting for us.

Throughout the night, prayer and stillness encompassed the room. With clarity and focus, we entreated God with our needs. Our requests were not random but precise and we could sense that God was answering.

It was a safe environment. We ladies were open to share and confess. James 5:16 says, "Therefore confess your sins to each other and pray for one another that you may be healed. The prayer of a righteous person is powerful and effective."

We were entrusted to one another's care…love, trust, confidentiality, peace, and fellowship. It was all there.

Through the night, the cries, words of praise, and even the silence seemed to demonstrate our desire to abide in Him deeper than ever.

For me, it was a great experience knowing that we are one in Him. His presence is so precious. His passion for us is great.

The scripture that night had a central theme 'abide'. "If you abide in me …" (John 15:7).

As we left the next morning, I have committed to memory how light and carefree I felt. I thank God for showing up.

Kathy Froitzheim
Bonita Springs, Florida

❖❖❖❖

CHAPTER ONE

Come Away My Beloved

My beloved spake, and said unto me,
Rise up, my love, my fair one, and
come away.
Song of Solomon 2:10 (KJV)

Women have a defining quality that allows them to bond with one another. We are social butterflies, and friendship is a vital part of our lives.

Unfortunately over a period of time, our solidarity with one another has been placed on the back burner. The shifts in our responsibilities have taken precedence.

From the moment we open our eyes in the morning, our minds are jam-packed with unattainable to-do lists. By the evening, our bodies are exhausted. We find ourselves with little to no energy to do anything else.

Whether we have discovered it or not, we all have at least one similar characteristic from either Mary or Martha. These two sisters are mentioned in Luke 10:40. Mary did not take it lightly that there were things that needed to be accomplished. But in the frenzy of the day, she considered it a privilege to pause and sit at Jesus' feet, gaining what could never be taken away.

On the other hand, Martha worried about what was not getting done. Her motive may have been in the right place, but her priorities were mislaid. Her feverish attempts to impress Jesus caused her to miss an opportunity to pause in His presence.

In neglect of our fellowship, we sometimes find out later rather than sooner the reason that we're feeling out of sorts. Somehow we have failed to remember what was important.

Like Martha, we focus on the minor instead of the major. Our intentions may be right, but how we go about it misses the mark. Could it be that we have disregarded our need for fellowship with our Savior and with one another?

Pausing in His presence provides us with times of refreshing that bring harmony and balance to our lives. This is a time where you will never be disappointed, it is a time where you gain what can never be taken away.

❖❖❖❖

What girl doesn't like to play with dolls? For most of my elementary school-age years, my plastic-toy friends became my confidants. As humorous as it sounds, I guess I had my first shut-in with these "ladies."

At the age of thirteen, I became the neighborhood babysitter, evolving from dolls to real-life children. As soon as I turned sixteen, I went out into the world with my babysitting skills in one hand and my working papers in the other. I acquired a summer job tutoring with the CETA (Comprehensive Employment and Training Act) Program. Some years later, my tutoring experience became helpful as I volunteered in children's ministries and various outreaches.

Up until this point, working with children became an undeclared lifelong ministry. The youth we had the privilege to mentor, were a welcomed addition to our family of seven. However after a number of years, I began to feel a prodding to place the mothers of these children, God's daughters; at the height of my list.

Contrary to many viewpoints, no woman is an island. Yes, you can bring home the bacon and even fry it up in the pan, nevertheless; we need one another. All of us have or are going through something. Single-handedly it is hard to grow when one is suffering in silence and/or drowning without life support.

My passion is fueled from being the middle child who was born between two brothers. I know firsthand how beneficial a healthy relationship with sisters and friends can be. As a young adult, I was blessed to have the opportunity to nurture a bond with my half-sister. The restoration of our relationship fuels my zeal to encourage one of God's magnificent creations (His daughters) every opportunity I can.

There are countless who have not experienced a healthy relationship with their earthly father, mother or siblings and thus find it difficult to relate to their heavenly Father. God is one who loves to restore, His Sons' death did that very thing. It connected us back to Him. Fellowship is one of the many reasons He extends an invitation to come away with Him. As we permit Him to pour His love, mercy and grace upon us, we in turn are able to dispense His compassion upon others.

God is calling us to come away, to pause in His presence and become familiar with His Word, His way and His will. Once we experience this part of His character, we then begin to look forward to being still. We come to the understanding that anytime we get to shut in with God is time well-spent.

> O My beloved, abide under the shelter of the lattice for I have betrothed you to Myself, and though you are sometimes indifferent toward Me, My love for you is at all times as a flame of fire. My ardor never cools. My longing for your love and affection is deep and constant.
>
> Tarry not for an opportunity to have more time to be alone with Me. Take it, though you leave the tasks at hand. Nothing will suffer. Things are of less importance than you think. Our time together is like a garden full of flowers, whereas the time you give to things is as a field full of stubble.
>
> --Frances J. Roberts,
> *Come Away My Beloved*

*Selah...**Pause** and **Think** About It*

What may be keeping you from coming away with Him?

_____

_____

_____

_____

_____

_____

_____

_____

_____

_____

_____

_____

_____

_____

_____

_____

_____

CHAPTER TWO

Awake

Wherefore he saith, Awake thou that sleepest, and arise from the dead, and Christ shall give thee light.

Ephesians 5:14 (KJV)

All the Women of the Bible is a book written by Herbert Lockyer. In it, he wrote that Christian women in particular present to the world morality, home, happiness, piety, domestic honesty, and full devotion to Christ. As morals become more lax and society degenerates, God-fearing wives and mothers are more than ever vital factors in the spiritual elevation of the nation.

A dichotomy confronts every woman today. One option consists of chasing pleasure, loving sin, exalting divorce, and perverting sex, all of which springs from the rejection of Christ. The other option is the noblest and most beneficial for our homes, our nation, and our church, namely that of God-inspired devotion. It centers on the home, the husband, the children, and the scriptures.

Moral laxity among girls today and the ever-increasing divorce rate with its progressive polygamy constitutes a call to continuous intercession. We intercede so that God will raise these soon-to-be women to the venerable heights He intended. In fact, He wanted this for all of the daughters of Eve.

In the early part of 2008, the Lord showed me a vision of women shutting in. Without providing details in their totality, He instructed me to extend an invitation.

Exodus 25:22 states, "And there He would commune with us from above the mercy seat …" God wanted to meet with His daughters. He had something to share.

I had a mental picture of a room occupied by a number of women. As the occupants in the room worshipped and lifted up their petitions, this room filled with His glory.

As time passed, the vision of the women gathering in no way dissipated; in fact it grew stronger. With gladness I did what Habakkuk 2:2 says. I wrote the vision on paper in an unpretentious fashion so that anyone could run with it [author paraphrased].

Each time I revisited my notes, I realized there were segments that I thought were unattainable. I was reminded of Matthew 19:26 that tells us "… but with man this is impossible, but with God all things are possible."

And so we stretched forth in faith, with the assurance that when God gives the vision, He grants the provision.

❖❖❖❖

Though not a single person can utter a word when exiting his or her mother's womb, all of us are born with an innate ability to pray. Prayer is simply God communicating with us and vice versa. But often, we make prayer more difficult than it really is.

It's a misconception that we need a certain type of vocabulary or a specific amount of words when we pray. In 1 Samuel 16:7, we are told that God is looking to see what is in the heart. He places high priority on conversing about these matters. However, He is just as interested in wanting to express how much He loves us.

❖❖❖❖

Surrounded by a group of Titus women, we set aside some time to pray and fast. We sought God for a date, time, and a place to gather.

The Lord prompted us that it was time to share the vision with my pastor. As the meeting came to a close, we were all united and agreed that this was an invitation from God. Remember I mentioned earlier, when God gives the vision, He will give the provision. My pastor provided us with his support, a location, and transportation.

The date was set and everything was paid in full. All that remained were the responses from the invitees.

Without ceasing prayer, praise, and thanksgiving became three constants. We stayed focused and tuned in to what the Lord had to say. With several weeks before the actual shut-in, God finally conveyed that He desired to break up the fallow ground.

Charles Finney, one of the most prominent revivalists during the Second Great Awakening in America, spoke about "What It Means to Break Up the Fallow Ground." He referred to fallow ground as terrain that has once been tilled but now lays wasted. It needs to be broken up before any seeds (the Word of God) can be planted.

There's a comparison of the mind of man to the ground, and an association of the Word of God to the sown seed. Today's culture has gone to great depths to entertain and engage our minds. Right is wrong, and wrong is right. Often our thoughts can ponder on what is contrary to the Word of God. What flows from our lives is evidence of what has been sown.

If the things of this world entertain us, in due season, our spirit man will wither away. But if you are engaged in the Word of God, and if you not only hear but hold fast to it, then be patient; you shall bear fruit (Luke 8:15).

When I think about breaking the fallow ground, my thoughts are taken back to a lady I met during an outreach at a homeless facility. The service had ended, and we were saying our goodbyes.

As I strolled to the exit door, she sat at a table all alone. I looked in her eyes and softly said, "God bless you."

She quickly replied, "Yes, He has. I know how good God is to me. My issue is I'm not good to myself."

I put my departure on hold to let her continue her story.

She went on to say that she wasn't here because of drugs, alcohol, or sexual abuse. Selfishness, being judgmental, and lacking compassion were what placed her here. She resided in this facility for unobvious reasons.

I had no verbal reply. All I could see was that she had placed herself in the Potter's hands. She was allowing God to break up her fallow ground. She found a place of refuge and deliberately paused so that she could be renewed.

As I prepared to leave, I embraced my new sister-friend and commended her courage. She, like Martha's sister Mary, sought a time of refreshing, a time where her soul could be revived and restored.

A lot of times in life as well as in ministry we think we're positioned in places to be a blessing. At the end of the day, we find out that God had something bigger planned. That evening when I settled down, I thanked Him for my newfound sister. I pondered on the fact that God desires to reach the dry places in each of our lives.

> "Two are better than one; because they have a good reward for their labour. [10]For if they fall, the one will lift up his fellow: but woe to him that is alone when he falleth; for he hath not another to help him up. [11]Again, if two lie together, then they have heat: but how can one be warm alone? [12]And if one prevail against him, two shall withstand him; and a threefold cord is not quickly broken" (Ecclesiastes 4:9–12).

In concluding a study on the book of Colossians, Brian Bill's stated in his sermon, "We're reminded that our faith should affect our friendships. Instead of just looking out for ourselves, we need to recognize that we really do need each other because we're all members of one body." Look around. We're encircled by women who need us. Look around for we are our sister's keeper.

❖❖❖❖

With the shut-in rapidly approaching, we discovered that this work of God could not be accomplished by any one individual. Whatever God may be calling any of us to do cannot be fulfilled without first His blessing and second, the support and prayers of others.

In 1 Corinthians 12, Paul shares with us how the church is designed to function. The Body of Christ is not just a group of religious people who get together. God has created us as many members with many gifts, all to be used for His glory.

There was no need to solicit for anything once the invitation was published, His daughters asked, "What can I do? What can I bring?"

Like Moses in Exodus 36, the people brought more than enough, and so it was with the preparations for the shut-in. Multitudes of people interceded while we planned and expected God to move mightily. We were just as hungry for God spiritually as we are for food in the natural.

The women entered the room, responding without delay. You could hear their whispers as they wondered what was about to take place. Excitement and curiosity filled the air as several communicated that they had no idea what to expect. I don't imagine any of us could pinpoint what God had in store. All we knew was that He made us an offer we could not refuse.

I surveyed the list to ensure all who signed up were in attendance. I was thrilled to see that there was an overflow.

The ladies' attention was requested and we directed them to the seating area where the seats were formed into a circle. After a time of introductions and icebreakers, we found ourselves enveloped in praise and worship.

I believed the best way to describe it was as if we were sitting in our Heavenly Father's lap. Over the next twenty hours, several women lined up to speak, all in agreement that God was in control, and we had come to hear what He had to say.

Pausing in His presence brought forth a time of breaking and birthing. Intercession was going forth from one end of the room to the other. It was as if we were lying on a labor-and-delivery floor. Several were surrounded with midwives who stayed and prayed them to their deliverance. On one end of the room, some were releasing what they had held onto for years, and on the other end, some were becoming alive for the first time.

After what seemed like only a short period of time, we found that we had been awake for hours. Wow, AWAKE that was the theme the Lord had given us, and awake we were. The ladies cried, laughed, and rejoiced in what the Lord had done for them.

With wisdom, we realized we were due to rise early the next morning. We made ourselves retire for the evening. The exhilaration didn't dim even as we lay upon our beds, the fellowship continued until the last person dozed off.

❖❖❖❖

What sounded like a snooze button was the buzz of anticipation for round two. We all rose with the morning sun. After breakfast, we ran to the meeting place for an extra serving.

One of our speakers of the day revealed God in the most intimate and personal way. In sharing more than a few of God's names, she illuminated His character and personality.

For most shut-ins, we set aside a quiet time to journal. At first some thought this to be a time where they were going to just jot down their prayer request and shut their book. But as we were logging our thoughts and prayers, God spoke. He instructed us to approach the microphone, to each stand front and center and make known our request to Him.

Several found this to be a challenge. We were going to have to reveal what others did not know. Many became anxious at the notion of this type of transparency. But obedience is so much better than sacrifice. The moment we stepped up, God met us. The minute we made our requests known, on that very spot, He reached out and touched us from Heaven. The burdens and the yokes that had caused several of the ladies to arrive hunched over no longer existed.

And so it is for you. God's invitation is extended to you. He wants to be your Healer, your Provider, your Shepherd, and your Friend.

26

*Selah...**Pause** and **Think** About It*

What area of your life is God trying to AWAKE?

_____

_____

_____

_____

_____

_____

_____

_____

_____

_____

_____

_____

_____

_____

_____

_____

_____

_____

_____

CHAPTER THREE

The Tabernacle: His Dwelling Place

> We will go into his tabernacles: we
> will worship at his footstool.
>
> ### *Psalms 132:7(KJV)*

The tabernacle is a means to the end. It's a representation of the several stages of a shut-in. Every facet of the tabernacle raises our awareness to the breadth, length, depth and height of His love. It reveals to us how one can have a satisfying relationship with God here on earth.

The tabernacle consists of three sections: the outer court, the inner court known as the Holy Place, and the Most Holy Place also known as the Holy of Holies.

Two out of the three areas contain a number of items, whereas the Holy of Holies has one. Upon entering the third section, you'll find that the closer one gets to God, the less one needs. The single most important element that is vital to our existence is Him.

Jesus' death on the cross over two thousand years ago was for you and me. His death removed the power of sin over and in our lives. His sacrifice built the bridge that mended our relationship with His Father.

There are things about Him and ourselves that we won't recognize, comprehend, and often address unless we are still. There is an exchange that takes place and it is important that the individual perceive what is happening. Pausing in His presence provides us with this opportunity. We're able to become familiar with Him, His will, and His ways.

The responsibility of entering in from the outer court is an individual choice. We have noticed that even though a person yearns to go further, the unknown causes them to park in the inner court. For others, the concerns of family, friends, and even life has paralyzed them. They refrain from crossing the threshold to the Holy of Holies.

While pausing in His presence, we don't look to change our circumstances and situations. Our perspective is what changes. As God meets us more than halfway, we find that His Word will sustain us. His will is what protects us, and His ways are best for us.

❖❖❖❖

The Merriam-Webster Dictionary defines tabernacle as a building for public worship and especially Christian worship.

In Exodus 28 and Hebrews 9 and 10, we see that God required the sacrifice of unblemished animals to be offered as a temporary covering of sins. Once a year on the Day of Atonement, the priest performed the duties that were described in the Old Testament. These offerings for the tabernacle also foreshadowed the perfect and complete sacrifice of Jesus Christ.

The blood of the Lamb of God ended the priests' sacrament. When the sinless Lamb of God, Jesus Christ, willingly died for us, He paid for our past, present, and future sins.

There's a message in the transition from the sacrifice of animals to the sacrificial substitute of Jesus. It implies that God no longer resides in a building but in a temple.

In 1 Corinthians 3:16–17, Paul says, "Know ye not that ye are the temple of God, and *that* the Spirit of God dwelleth in you? [17]If any man defile the temple of God, him shall God destroy; for the temple of God is holy, which *temple* ye are."

What Jesus did is for you and me. Now we can go boldly before the throne of God to obtain His grace and mercy, especially in our time of need. Because of the mercy of God, Paul beseeched us in Romans 12:1–2 to present our bodies as a living sacrifice, holy and acceptable unto God. This *is* our reasonable service.

We are not to be *conformed* to this world but *transformed* by the renewing of our mind so that we may prove what *is* the good, the acceptable, and the perfect will of God (author paraphrase from Romans 12:2). God's Word transforms. As we allow the Holy Spirit to inhabit our temple, we become a living sacrifice unto God.

In his overview of the Book of Exodus, Ray Stedman states the worse thing we can do is teach that the building is the house of God. He believes that God wants us to learn that we are never out of church and that Jesus Christ Himself is dwelling in our body, which is His temple.

Our body is built exactly like the tabernacle. It has a threefold structure. The outer court is of flesh and bones which we see. The holy place is the soul—the realms of emotions, mind, and will. This is the area from which we can interact with one with another. It's the area that gives us the inclination to talk and share experiences together.

Deep at the center is the Holy of Holies, which represents our spirit. In that place, the Spirit of God dwells.

Therefore, each of us is a walking tabernacle.

❖❖❖❖

So what does the tabernacle have to do with a shut-in?

The tabernacle is a representation of the several stages of a shut-in. It's more than having a theme, a guest speaker, or refreshments; it's about responding to the invitation from God to come and commune with Him. By entering into the gate, you have made a purposeful endeavor to have a dialogue with God.

This allegoric illustration provides a glimpse of the intimate time of fellowship that takes place in a shut-in. It's a journey that challenges one to pause and take inventory of their lives.

Courage is needed to enter through the gate from the outer court and lay the issues of the heart upon the brazen altar. We're posed with many questions, such as; are we willing to be transparent so that we can be cleansed by the water in the laver.

One of my favorite places and the height of the shut-in experience is the Most Holy Place, also known as the Holy of Holies. The invitation we received was not so that we could come and be entertained but that we could come and have an exchange. Pausing in His presence reminds us of His promises, purposes, provision, pardon, and protection.

I believe that many are yearning to enter into the Holy of Holies, but there is a hesitation. Could it be that the enemy of one's soul would have them believe he or she isn't worthy? This is partly right; we're not. Only because of the blood of Jesus, which washes away all of our sins, has He made us worthy.

Come boldly from outside and into the courtyard because God has invited you. He is standing at the door excited about spending time with His creation. The time we spend pausing in His presence will provide spiritual blessings that can not be purchased.

Beloved, God is calling you to come away, though you may feel like you will lose something. God promises to meet you, speak to you, and give you what cannot be taken away.

*Selah...**Pause** and **Think** About It*

Take inventory of your relationship with God and with others.

_____

_____

_____

_____

_____

_____

_____

_____

_____

_____

_____

_____

_____

_____

_____

_____

_____

_____

_____

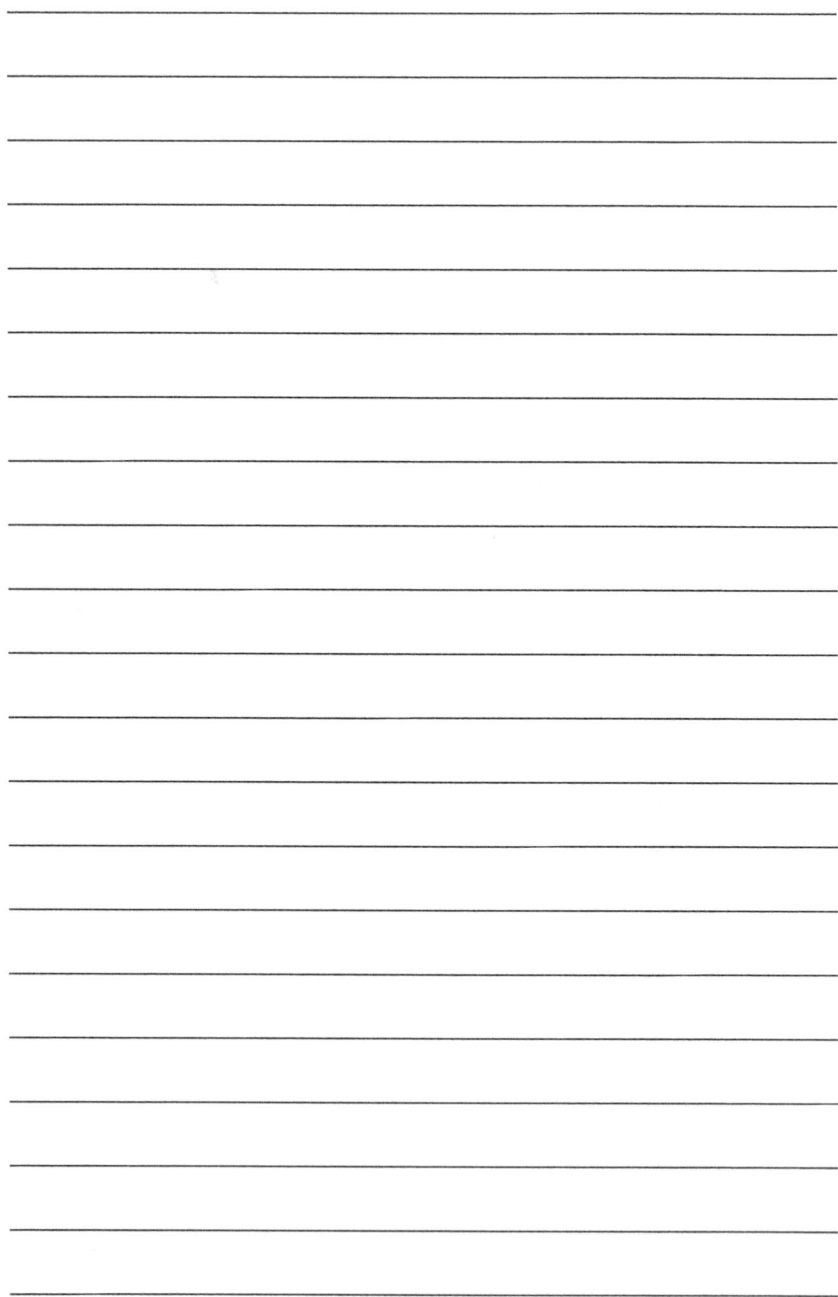

Chapter Four

The Gate

Behold, I stand at the door, and knock:
if any man hear My voice, and open
the door, I will come in to him, and
will sup with him, and he with Me.

Revelation 3:20 (KJV)

Watching a child's energy when he senses his parents are nearby is a wonderful sight. They don't have to physically see them. Some babies have such a keen sense of smell that causes them to become aware of their relative's approach without even hearing their voices.

It has been noted that the gate represents Jesus Christ, and we, God's creation, stand on the outer court. Jesus is calling His creation to enter in and commune with Him. But oftentimes, we miss His invitation because we didn't sense His presence, nor did we recognize His voice.

❖❖❖❖

Fully aware that God is in control, we rely on His wisdom and prepare for each shut-in. Assembling the praise and worship music is on the top of the checklist. Often I found myself spending just as much time coordinating the music as I spent in prayer.

For this particular shut-in, I was made aware of some new artist and hurriedly burned a CD. Prior to this night, I was not aware of the different types of compact discs. The variations in the CD's which are available in both write-once audio and data storage (CD-R) and rewritable media (CD-RW) often make them incapable of being played in any given hard drive and/or CD player.

After what I thought was a successful burn, I left earlier than usual and made my way to the meeting place for the shut-in. I entered the building and made a bee line to the equipment booth. I couldn't wait to hear the new tunes on the church's sound system.

I was fumbling with the CD player as the ladies began to arrive. Seeing that I was preoccupied with a technical difficulty, one of the ladies graciously volunteered to man the door and welcome the attendees. As I popped the CD in and out of the player, a red *reader error* message flashed on the screen. A few minutes later, I paused as the Holy Spirit instructed me to leave it alone. Though I was determined to find a way to make it work, I knew it was time to surrender.

God had His own agenda. He wanted a time of pure worship,

one that came from our hearts and not from a CD.

God also has a humorous side. Later in the evening as we basked in His presence and in His Word, one of the ladies located a portable compact disc player in one of the back rooms. She inserted a CD and hit play. We allowed a few selections to play before turning it off.

Sitting around the altar in silence, we individually lifted our hearts in prayer. The atmosphere was serene. No one talked or looked around.

All of a sudden, out of the blue and without any human assistance, the CD player lit up. The lyrics softly played, "We pour out our miseries. God hears a melody. Beautiful the mess we are. The honest cries of breaking hearts are better than a hallelujah."

We then heard another sound, and we all looked up to find the source. We saw it was someone crying.

Little did anyone know, but in her quiet time, a shut-in member had asked the Lord if He loved her, and if He did, could He give her a sign. This song titled "Better than a Hallelujah" by Amy Grant was an answer to her prayer. Though she was in misery, God was the only one who heard her breaking heart, and it was better than a hallelujah.

The rest of us sat in awe and were humbled as we were given a gentle reminder that God does not need our help. All He needs is our availability and willingness to respond.

*Selah...**Pause** and **Think** About It*

What could be keeping you from hearing His voice?

_____

_____

_____

_____

_____

_____

_____

_____

_____

_____

_____

_____

_____

_____

_____

_____

CHAPTER FIVE

The Brazen Altar

And Jesus answered them, saying, The hour is come, that the Son of man should be glorified. [24] Verily, verily, I say unto you, Except a corn of wheat fall into the ground and die, it abideth alone: but if it die, it bringeth forth much fruit. [25] He that loveth his life shall lose it; and he that hateth his life in this world shall keep it unto life eternal.

John 12:23–25 (KJV)

The Tabernacle consisted of two altars, the Brazen Altar and the Altar of Incense. The Brazen Altar, also known as the Bronze Altar, located in the outer court. The Altar of Incense, also known as the Golden Altar of Incense, rested in the Holy Place, which was the inner court.

In the Old Testament, a ritual performed by the priest on the altar was one of continual bloodshed. An animal without blemish or spot was killed and presented to God as a pardon for the sins of the people. However when the perfect Lamb—Jesus Christ—shed His blood, His death put an end to this Old Testament ceremony.

Christ came as a high priest of good things to come. He came by a greater and more perfect tabernacle, not made with human hands. By His own blood He entered once and for all into the Holy Place and secured complete eternal redemption for us (Hebrews 9:11–12 AMP).

The priest had an enormous responsibility. Their duties included the day-to-day functions and rituals in addition to the animal sacrifices. They served as mediators of God's presence.

Most of what the priest did pertained to outward acts. What the blood of Christ did and still does today is a work from the inside out.

Jesus' life is the perfect example of a sacrifice full of grace and mercy. His death, burial, and resurrection can help us relate to the transition that takes place in one's shut-in experience. We will die, be buried, but hold on; resurrection is next for we cannot truly live until we have utterly died.

The journey through the tabernacle requires action. We will be required to bury what is hindering our relationship with God.

We cannot expect to enjoy God's promises without living out His purposes for our lives. Like Jesus, we must desire God's will more than our own. When we surrender, the Holy Spirit can do an inside job. Once our sinful man is burned upon the Brazen Altar, His work liberates us and we begin to see and experience the resurrected life of Christ.

❖❖❖❖

Like most youth back in my day, we grew up playing a game called Pick Up Sticks. Its original name was Mikado and was created in Europe. In 1936, it was brought from Hungary to the United States. Playing this game required physical and mental skill.

First, the Pick Up Sticks were tossed onto a solid surface, creating a loose pile. The tricky part and object of the game was for a player to end up with the most sticks without disturbing the remaining ones.

Like Pick Up Sticks, we toss our burdens into a pile upon the altar. Society is screaming to go ahead, grab and take them all back. But God is trying to show us that it's in our best interest to leave some of the sticks alone. Unfortunately, in an attempt to grab what we think we need, we give in to temptation and disturb the pile.

More times than not, this is due to our lack of knowledge. We have become comfortable with the familiar and afraid of the unknown. We have not fully understood that in order to advance to the Holy of Holies, we must leave some of the sticks where they lay for those are the very things that must die in order for us to live.

❖❖❖❖

At the closing of Sunday morning services after first receiving Jesus as my Savior, I became a permanent fixture at the altar. As a babe in Christ, I picked up my burdens from Monday through Saturday. On Sunday, I laid them down again.

This recurring behavior continued until one day, a friend intervened. Services were coming to a close, and I began to move toward the altar.

My friend gently grabbed my hand and whispered, "You don't need to keep going to the front. You're saved. What you need to do is live like it."

Her loving rebuke showed me my responsibility or lack thereof. I had the religious part down but was missing a relationship with God. I knew how to do the church thing but didn't have what I needed to live like a Christian; I needed Christ's power on the inside. I needed to commune with Him.

While I'm not trying to tear down any religion, the fact remains that religions are manmade and full of rituals. Several religions are based upon trying to get to God through rules, regulations, and works. God's plan is not based on our efforts but on His amazing love, mercy, and grace.

At the Brazen Altar, our flesh has been put to death so that we might live. In due season, we come to understand that God isn't asking us to surrender anything that we can't do without. He is with us and will provide everything we need so that we might have life and have it abundantly.

*Selah...**Pause** and **Think** About It*

What is God asking you to lay down?

_____

_____

_____

_____

_____

_____

_____

_____

_____

_____

_____

_____

_____

_____

_____

_____

_____

_____

_____

CHAPTER SIX

The Brazen Laver

Jesus knowing that the Father had given all things into His hands, and that He was come from God, and went to God; ⁴He riseth from supper, and laid aside His garments; and took a towel, and girded Himself. ⁵After that He poureth water into a basin, and began to wash the disciples' feet, and to wipe them with the towel wherewith He was girded. ... ¹²So after He had washed their feet, and had taken His garments, and was set down again, He said unto them, know ye what I have done to you? ¹³Ye call me Master and Lord: and ye say well: for so I am. ¹⁴If I then, your Lord and Master, have washed your feet; ye also ought to wash one another's feet. ¹⁵For I have given you an example that ye should do as I have done to you.

John 13:3–5, 12–15 (KJV)

It is difficult to know where you're going without having some knowledge of where you've been. This fragment of information can be instrumental in encouraging or discouraging you from who God created you to be.

Jesus knew from where He came. This didn't make Him conceited but gave Him an assurance of where He was going. His relationship with His Father allowed Him to recognize that no matter what He was to endure, there was a purpose in it.

Our Savior was able to see and accept His God-given purpose because He had spent time pausing in His presence. He had consistent fellowship with God. When life on earth began getting hectic, Jesus went directly to His Father.

The Brazen Laver is a large basin filled with water. The water in the laver is known to symbolize the Bible. "The Word of God is quick and powerful, and sharper than any two-edged sword, piercing even to the dividing asunder of soul and spirit, and of the joints and marrow, and is a discerner of the thoughts and intents of the heart" (Hebrews 4:12 KJV).

The issues of the heart are uncovered. Here at the Brazen Laver, God desires to wash you white as snow. The washing of one's hands or feet are ceremonial, but a cleansing of the heart is essential.

At the Brazen Laver, the Word of God examines the intentions of our heart. A sifting occurs. Right and wrong thoughts, habits, and motives are either purified or purged.

At the Laver, we are bathed. We put on the mind of Christ. We desire to live out our lives for the glory of God. His love for us has been made plain and simple. What He has done for us, we now have a desire for others to experience.

If you have come this far, you recognize that it is only because of God's riches at Christ's' expense. There are no short cuts, in order to advance to the Holy of Holies; time at the Brazen Laver is a must.

❖❖❖❖

Notice there is a separation from what would contaminate our relationship with God. We were forgiven and freed from sin at the Brazen Altar. A desire to live holy has been set in motion at the Brazen Laver. We are awaken to the fact that we live in the world, but no longer do we have to partake of everything the world has to offer.

In the movie *The Second Chance*, a man named Tony had lived his life in the streets. Tony was beaten up something awful for helping a young boy named Julius break free from an unlawful lifestyle.

Days passed, and the youth were preparing to go camping. Sonny the church custodian was hoping his newfound buddy Tony was going to be able to make it. Even though he had some serious injuries, Tony showed up much to their surprise.

As they were loading the bus, Sonny accidentally hit Tony's injured leg. Without thinking, the pain caused Tony to reply with one of his typical knee-jerk reactions.

Without any regard to the pain he caused, Sonny judged Tony for using what he defined as a cuss word. He quickly replied, "Tony, God doesn't like it when you swear."

Days later when they returned from the camping trip, they were participating in a Bible study in the church's sanctuary. Sonny made a confession. He shared that he had read in his Bible where Jesus did something special for his best friends.

Sonny humbled himself and washed Tony's feet. He asked him for forgiveness for judging him and for worrying about what he had said instead of how he had felt.

The combination of the altar and the laver will humble us. It is clear that we too have sinned and fallen short of God's glory.

*Selah...**Pause** and **Think** About It*

Examine the intents of your heart.

_____

_____

_____

_____

_____

_____

_____

_____

_____

_____

_____

_____

_____

_____

_____

_____

_____

_____

_____

CHAPTER SEVEN

The Inner Court~ The Holy Place

> And after the second veil, the tabernacle which is called the Holiest of all;
>
> **Hebrews 9:3 (KJV)**

The word *inner* means to move closer, to go deeper.

The articles in the outer court were made of brass. Brass represents the earthly man. Like brass, man is known to tolerate a certain amount of stress before he begins to crack.

From the outside looking in, it appears that we have it all together. But there are seasons in our lives when from the inside looking out, we are about to break.

In the outer court, confession and cleansing are two essential components that create a thirst for God. There is a stirring, an awakening. We yearn to move closer, to go deeper in Christ. We will not be satisfied until He inhabits the core of our souls.

The inner court, also known as the Holy Place, is located directly ahead of the outer court and just before the Holy of Holies.

In the Holy Place, we find three pieces of furnishings—the Table of Showbread, the Golden Lampstand, and the Golden Altar of Incense. All of these items are made of gold.

In the Holy Place, God confirms that He is still in our midst. Romans 8:28 says that He will work all things out for the good to them that love Him, to them who are called according to His purpose.

God requests to feed us through His word. He wishes to strengthen us through His Spirit. He desires to teach us His purposes through our prayers.

As we shift from the outer court to the Holy Place, there should be a conversion similar to that of the refining of gold. There is a process that we must endure if we are to be successful in our Christian walk. The Holy Place is where we allow our creator to do just that.

Gold's purification process has a spiritual implication. Gold is solid yet flexible. It never rusts and is not manmade. It's known for its rarity, firmness, and pliability. Gold can be crushed and twisted into all kinds of different shapes without breaking apart.

Another inference is described in Jeremiah 18:1–4. Here we are reminded that we are in the Potter's hands.

If you have ever watched a potter at their wheel, you'll notice they begin with a round, moist lump of clay. The clay's body is thrown down onto the wheel and centrifugal force is applied until no more roughness is felt.

The potter's thumb is pressed into the center of the lump to make a hole to the potter's measurements. The sides are molded, and the vessel is smoothened and shaped. The item is then cut from the wheel and left to stiffen.

Nothing can prepare one for the potter's wheel. In His hands we may think that we're physically dying at times, but death is a must if we're to live abundantly in Christ.

In this subdivision of the shut-in, time is not of the importance. There is no timetable for God needs to have free reign to shape us and make us into His likeness.

In the Holy Place, we come to the understanding that we won't make it; we cannot be victorious within our own ability. We need the help of the Lord.

Matthew 19:26 reminds us that with man it is impossible, but with God, all things are possible. It's impossible for us to save ourselves. But as we remain flexible in His hands, we shall come forth in ways that are so much better than we could have ever imagined.

*Selah...**Pause** and **Think** About It*

What does God desire to refine in you?

_____

_____

_____

_____

_____

_____

_____

_____

_____

_____

_____

_____

_____

_____

_____

_____

_____

CHAPTER EIGHT

The Golden Lampstand

Let your light so shine before men,
that they may see your good works,
and glorify our Father in Heaven.

Matthew 5:16 (KJV)

In the Holy Place, the lampstand is the only source of light. It burned continuously and lit the pathway to the other items in the room.

Made of pure gold, the lampstand had one shaft in the center and six branches, three on each side. The center shaft symbolized Jesus Christ, who is to be the center of our lives. The six branches on the side personified Christians. Like the center shaft that supported the lampstand, Jesus is our support system who raises us up so that we can shed light throughout this world.

As with the different wattages of a lightbulb, so it is with each of us. We are different yet alike. We are individuals, each producing a distinct lighting effect.

You and I may not be able to reach the same people, but we all should have the same goal and the same purpose. Our light should so shine that others can find their way to Him.

Day in and day out, we are to be observant of our surroundings. We are given many opportunities to be a light. God will show us those who need an encouraging word or even a cup of water.

Jesus said we are to be the light of the world, one that cannot be hidden. Our light will shine only to the depth of our relationship with Him. Our vertical relationship with Christ reflects our horizontal relationship with one another.

Just as He has lit the room for you, He desires you to do the same for someone else. If our fellowship with God is lacking, so will the outcome of our light. As we allow Him to be the center, we become a lighthouse that delights to share with others what we have inherited from God (author paraphrased 2 Corinthians 1:3–7).

❖❖❖❖

Remember the fictional movie *Pinocchio*? A lonely carpenter named Geppetto made a wooden puppet shaped like a boy. They enjoyed each other's company so much that Geppetto wished upon a falling star for the puppet to become an actual child.

The star then returned to Geppetto in the form of a blue

fairy. She told them what she would do for them and advised what they needed to do to make the wish come true.

If Pinocchio wanted to become a real boy, he had to prove himself to be brave, truthful, and unselfish. Like us, he had to go through a season that would both test and shape his character.

Pinocchio had to learn to tell right from wrong by listening to his conscience. However, he didn't have a clue as to what a conscience was.

To assist him with his transition, the fairy appointed Jiminy Cricket, a comical and wise partner. He excitedly accepted the task to supply Pinocchio with the guidance needed to behave decently and honorably.

Have you considered that perhaps God has anointed and appointed you to be a Lamaze partner to a sister-friend? Have you thought that by becoming a Jiminy Cricket to someone, you can help birth them into their destiny? Providing support for them to become all that God has created them to be.

During his move from one adventure to another, the inexperienced Pinocchio ignored the warnings from Jiminy. Like Pinocchio, the very one you are trying to help may stray on a number of occasions, but so did we at one time or another. We must not give up on them because God, full of His grace and mercy, did not give up on us.

Finding himself in one bad situation after another, Pinocchio didn't come to his senses until he was told that his father was in danger.

The reality of his situation hit him. His love for his father awakened his conscious and caused him to devise a plan to save his dad and prove himself trustworthy.

This is what I believe each of us is called to do. With the Lord's guidance and direction, we are to take a sister by the hand and walk the journey with her. We're not to release her until she is securely in the hands of our Father or if for some reason the Lord instructs us to let go.

There was a period of time when Jiminy Cricket left Pinocchio on his own. Unfortunately there will be times when we too must release our sisters. God does not force anyone to love Him, and neither should we. Like Pinocchio who had to be awakened to what was important to him, it is an individual thing for one to come to the knowledge of the love of God.

Most of us have had a Jiminy Cricket at some point along the way. We've had someone who was a constant in our lives until we latched onto the Comforter, the One who never leaves us or forsakes us.

We have a lot in common with Pinocchio. Jesus did for us in real life what this Jiminy Cricket did for Pinocchio in this story.

Jesus prayed to His Father to give us His Holy Spirit so that we won't walk around aimlessly in the dark. So we can be confident in the fact that even when no one is physically there for us, Jesus is always there. He will comfort, guide and instruct us in the way we should go.

While there could be many reasons why you are reading this book, let the main one be for you to receive revelation from God, may His purpose and plan for your life be crystal clear. May you allow the Lord to light your candle and use you for His glory that you may shine so that others might see and come to know Him.

*Selah...**Pause** and **Think** About It*

Where might your light be needed?

_____

_____

_____

_____

_____

_____

_____

_____

_____

_____

_____

_____

_____

_____

_____

_____

CHAPTER NINE

The Table of Showbread

I am the true vine, and my Father is
the husbandman. ²Every branch in me
that beareth not fruit He taketh away:
and every branch that beareth fruit,
He purgeth it, that it may bring forth
more fruit. ³Now ye are clean through
the word which I have spoken unto
you. ⁴Abide in Me, and I in you. As
the branch cannot bear fruit of itself,
except it abide in the vine; no more
can ye, except ye abide in Me. ⁵I am
the vine, ye are the branches: He that
abideth in me, and I in him, the same
bringeth forth much fruit: for without
Me ye can do nothing .

John 15:1–5 (KJV)

The family dinner hour is known to be one of the main ingredients in building a strong family. A distinct and most effective way for a family to be engaged in one another's life is to break bread together.

Gallup polls combined for 2001, 2005, and 2013 find that family dining hasn't diminished much in the recent years. It continues to be a part of everyday life. Fifty-three percent of adults with children younger than eighteen years of age say their family eats dinner together at home six or seven nights a week.

As a youngster our family regularly ate together. Dinner was ready about the same time every evening. This was a time we by and large looked forward to. I look at it as another way to fellowship. My mom worked forty hours a week and still found time, from Monday through Thursday; to cook a full meal, which always included a dessert.

She as well must have known how important it was to eat dinner together. Friday and Saturday were set aside for sandwiches or take out. Sunday meals were restaurant-style and cooked in a matchless 'mom' manner.

From Genesis to Revelation, we can see how it's worth holding on to some traditions. Not knowing any different, I included this pattern of behavior in my home with my own family. Dinner together was often a time to relax, laugh, and tell stories. However, as our children began to transition into young adults, schedules changed. Finding time for one another became challenging.

Today as each of our children reside in their own homes, we are blessed when we catch a glimpse that this tradition still exists. It is in the best interest of every family and/or person to form some type of habitual fellowship. Being in the presence of one another causes iron to sharpen iron. This is a time where matters of the heart can be discovered and life lessons can be shared.

Breaking bread together must not become extinct. It is an indispensable practice that should remain if the family, as God intended, is to survive.

In the inner court on the right-hand side of the Holy Place and opposite from the Lampstand stood the Table of Showbread. The King James Version spells showbread as "shewbread," which means "bread of the Presence." This represents that we can without fail remain in the presence of the Lord.

As the Tabernacle was a representation of what was coming through Jesus Christ, the Table of Showbread represents that Jesus is the bread of life. He is the bread of God from Heaven who gives life unto the world (John 6:33–35). He has come so that we shall never hunger again.

It's the same with family fellowship. In most cases when it's cultivated the right way, it will satisfy even the hungriest of souls.

In the day of so many gadgets and the frenzy of multi-tasking, we tend to have a one-way hurried conversation with God. We have the audacity to expect Him to hear us and move quickly. We have turned our prayers into wish list. We have become like a toddler at His feet pleading, "Gimme, gimme, gimme."

We don't have a problem making time for God when we're desperately in need of something. It's hard to envision that we have someone who has died to spend time with us. Yet we oftentimes have to be near death to spend time with Him.

At the Table of Showbread, God has given us an open-ended invitation to commune with Him. His table provides more than material blessings. There's a shower of peace, wisdom, knowledge, and understanding of Him as well as oneself.

Jesus Christ wants us to know that fellowship with Him is so much more than answered prayer. He desires to feed us and nurture us so that when the issues of life come our way, we'll have what we need.

He's calling us to His table. There's a seat reserved for you, will you join Him?

*Selah...**Pause** and **Think** About It*

What are some ways you can have fellowship
with the Lord and with others?

_____

_____

_____

_____

_____

_____

_____

_____

_____

_____

_____

_____

_____

_____

_____

_____

_____

_____

CHAPTER TEN

The Golden Altar of Incense

I exhort therefore, that, first of all, supplications, prayers, intercessions, and giving of thanks, be made for all men; [2]For kings, and for all that are in authority; that we may lead a quiet and peaceable life in all godliness and honesty.

1 Timothy 2:1–2 (KJV)

At the Table of Showbread, we saw that God's presence no longer resides in a building but in us. Being recipients of fresh manna on a daily basis, we can then give to others in return. We have freely received; we freely give (Matthew 10:8).

At this juncture, the Golden Altar of Incense brings to light how Jesus, our High Priest, continually prays to God on our behalf. Visualize Jesus sitting next to His Father, leaning over to Him, conversing to God about us. Jesus offering up prayers to God on our behalf is an example of how we are to intercede for one another.

There are many scriptures in the Bible that instruct us on how we are to pray for each other. In Ephesians 6:18, Paul says to pray at all times … for all of the saints. One of my favorite scriptures is Ephesians 3:14–19 where Paul prays for every family in heaven and on earth. He prays that God may grant them what they need so that they will be rooted and grounded in love. He prays for them to be strengthened with all of the saints so that they can comprehend who God really is (author paraphrased).

Intercession is a serious matter. Though intercession is a time of bringing our needs and the needs of others to God, it is so much more.

The word intercession and incense are intertwined. It's the love of God that brings us to our knees to pray for someone other than ourselves. Paul exhorts us in 1 Timothy 2:1 to "… first of all, supplications, prayers, intercessions, and giving of thanks, be made for all men."

In order to make praying for others a priority, we must first take care of our business in the outer court. If our prayers are to rise to the nostrils of God, we ourselves must die to self and be awaken to His will.

Interceding for others requires that we lose our will, our desires, and even our time. We must never pray for our will to be done. Our prayers should always be for the glory of God and for the benefit of those for whom we are praying.

Christ's' prayers were and still are a method of intervention and a time of prevention on our behalf. When prayed His way, our prayers cannot help but become a sweet-smelling aroma to God.

In his devotion on intercessory prayer, Oswald Chambers stated that true intercession is bringing the person or circumstance before God. We should do this until we are changed by His attitude toward that person or circumstance. "Men ought always to pray and not faint" (Luke 18:1).

Our prayers should ignite the incense that is burned continually on the Golden Altar. But in order for us to truly intercede through prayer, we must believe in the reality of redemption. If we don't, then we'll simply be turning intercession into useless sympathy for others.

There is nothing new under the sun. It's still the same as it was when Jesus walked this earth. We all will endure some suffering in our lifetime, which can cause us to feel overwhelmed by the requests and needs of others.

True intercession is not putting yourself in someone's place. We are to pray until the burden has been lifted. We should pray until confidence rises within us. Our prayer should continue without ceasing until we believe and have the will of God etched in our spirit.

Intercession is putting yourself in God's place. It's having His mind and His perspective. Sometimes we are burdened because we have our own opinions of how things should go. We are to continue in prayer until our attitude and our will line up with His.

The work of an intercessor is to be in such close contact with God that we can have His mind about everything. In interceding for others, we must avoid praying for someone to be simply "patched up." We must pray that this person comes in contact with the very life of God.

1 John 5:14 give us the blessed assurance that as long as we are praying according to His will, God has heard and will do what we have asked.

❖❖❖❖

Of all the things that one of the disciples could have asked Jesus, they chose to ask Him to teach them how to pray.
In Luke 11:1–5, Jesus provided us with Prayer 101. He didn't leave any of us who have read this text uninformed of how to pray.

> And it came to pass, that, as He was praying in a certain place, when He ceased, one of His disciples said unto him, Lord, teach us to pray, as John also taught his disciples. ²And He said unto them, When ye pray, say, Our Father which art in heaven, Hallowed be thy name. Thy kingdom come. Thy will be done, as in heaven, so in earth. ³Give us day by day our daily bread. ⁴And forgive us our sins; for we also forgive every one that is indebted to us. And lead us not into temptation; but deliver us from evil.

Notice that even in this text, intercession is occurring. He is praying for our Father to give us our daily bread, to forgive us, to lead us not into temptation, and to deliver us.

We can say so much to God, but in this scripture Jesus is teaching us how to address God as our Father. We are to acknowledge His Kingdom and His will.

We may not get everything we want, but we will have everything we need. He goes on with a self-explanatory caution: how can we ask God to forgive us if we don't forgive others?

Finally with the realization that God protects us from unseen danger, we can thank God for His leading us out of temptation and delivering us from the evil one.

He is truly worthy to be praised for His provision, providence, and protection are ours for the asking.

*Selah...**Pause** and **Think** About It*

Pray for someone.

_____

_____

_____

_____

_____

_____

_____

_____

_____

_____

_____

_____

_____

_____

_____

CHAPTER ELEVEN

The Holy of Holies Behind The Torn Veil

Having therefore, brethren, boldness to enter into the holiest by the blood of Jesus, [20]By a new and living way, which He hath consecrated for us, through the veil, that is to say, His flesh; [21]And having an high priest over the house of God; [22]Let us draw near with a true heart in full assurance of faith, having our hearts sprinkled from an evil conscience, and our bodies washed with pure water.

Hebrews 10:19–22 (KJV)

We were created to bring glory to God. As you pause, consider how you're blessed to be a blessing.

Released in 1999, self-described literary writer Catherine Ryan Hyde had a breakthrough novel called *Pay It Forward.* It quickly became a national bestseller and was later adapted into the film *Pay It Forward*, which was released in 2000.

According to published interviews, the idea for the novel was birthed when Catherine's car caught fire in what she described as the "bad neighborhood" where she lived. Two total strangers came to her assistance and then left before she could even thank them.

Pay It Forward Day is about people from all walks of life giving to someone else and making a positive difference. One simple deed can alter a person's life.

Isn't that what Jesus did? He lived a life that made a difference in every person He met.

The Old Testament shows us how the high priests were the only ones permitted to touch the veil. This veil separated the Holy Place from the Holy of Holies.

The veil represented the sins that have separated us from God. The priest performed a ritual that covered the nation's sins from the judgment of God and provided His forgiveness. This custom was conducted until the death of Jesus.

A price was to be paid. It was paid in full with the death of Christ.

Jesus went before God as our representative. He put Himself in our place, acting as our priest.

His death brought down the curtain. His blood paid the price. His life settled our debt once and for all.

> And Jesus cried out again with a
> loud voice, and yielded up His spirit.
> [51]Then, behold, *the veil* of the temple

was torn in two from top to bottom;
and the earth quaked, and the rocks
were split.

Matthew 27:50–51 (KJV)

No longer is it necessary for a priest to go to God on our behalf. Jesus' death tore the veil to the Holy of Holies, and animal sacrifices were no longer required. The death of Christ gave us access into this special dwelling place of God.

Jesus Christ had paid it forward. He paid the ultimate price once and for all. His death exposed the very presence of God, and He became available to everyone.

Jesus has paid it all. All to Him we owe.

❖❖❖❖

The most important benefit we received from the tearing of the veil is that we can now come and hear directly from God. He desires to have a conversation with us. He longs to converse with us.

If you can, pause and find a mirror. Turn your head from side to side and observe your reflection. Notice the number of ears and mouth you have.

Though God gave man more ears than He did mouths, listening has become a lost art. Here in the Holy of Holies, God is doing most of the talking, and we ought to be actively listening. Our shut-in event is not for our entertainment and is more than an occurrence. It's a time to pause and listen to God. An exchange has to take place in our mind, body, and soul. As we pay special attention to Him, we'll find ourselves submitting to a swap of our will for His.

*Selah...**Pause** and **Think** About It*

What do you need to swap so that you can draw near?

_____

_____

_____

_____

_____

_____

_____

_____

_____

_____

_____

_____

_____

_____

CHAPTER TWELVE

The Mercy Within The Ark

Then the cloud covered the tent of the congregation, and the glory of the LORD filled the tabernacle. And Moses was not able to enter into the tent of the congregation, because the cloud abode thereon, and the glory of the LORD filled the tabernacle.

Exodus 40:34–35 (KJV)

In the center of the Holy of Holies we find the Ark of the Covenant. It's the only piece of furniture in this section of the Tabernacle. The ark contains the mercy seat.

The beauty of His mercy is that we are recipients of it because of what Christ has done. It's not extended to us because of anything we've done. God's mercy is more than we deserve.

In Exodus 25:10–22, God gave instructions to build the Ark of the Covenant. He said, "In the ark you shall put the Testimony that I will give you. And there I will meet with you, and I will speak with you from above the mercy seat, from between the two cherubim which are on the ark of the Testimony, about everything which I will give you in commandment to the children of Israel."

A noteworthy fact in this section of the tabernacle is that there is no lamp or artificial lighting. God's glory is what illuminates the room.

The Holy of Holies is the ultimate goal for every shut-in. Action on our part begins from the very entrance of the outer court. With every step, your surrender fuels your determination that nothing and no one will keep you from receiving what God has in store for you. The presence of God is waiting for you. In the Holy of Holies, God is there with both arms wide open; ready to commune with you.

You laid it all upon the Bronze Altar. You dealt with what was concealed. You are now able to see yourself as He sees you. You are becoming who God created you to be: image bearers for His glory.

The plan is that His glory in you will draw others to Him. In due season, they'll inquire about what they must do to be adopted as His child. After being processed and molded, they will; do the same for others.

From the beginning of creation, God has never kept His desire to fellowship with us a secret. In spite of our sinful nature and continued disobedience, He remains faithful. His love, mercy, and grace have been showered upon us numerous times.

Thank God that He stepped in on our behalf and gave us His Son Jesus. He walked amongst us on this earth to have fellowship with you and me.

He set things decent and in order so that you and I can pause in His presence. Beloved, God is calling you, He has an unrelenting desire to sup with you…won't you come!

*Selah...**Pause** and **Think** About It*

What has God revealed to you?

_____

_____

_____

_____

_____

_____

_____

_____

_____

_____

_____

_____

_____

_____

_____

AFTERWORD

Pausing in His Presence is not confined to any geographical, economic, social, or denominational barriers. The inquisitive are not remaining on the outer court. They are firmly fixed on what is needed as they make their way to the Holy of Holies.

With each shut-in, no matter how many times one takes the journey from the outer court to the Holy of Holies, the passage is never the same. There are many testimonies, which women have given that they have come away with an unforeseen encounter with God. The only perquisite is that we avail ourselves. We are not only refreshed and revived but released to engage in the work of the Lord.

. ❖❖❖❖

My journey began in July 2008; the first shut in titled Awake consisted of thirty-five women. We shut in and shut down with God for more than twenty-four hours.

Several months later, we travelled to Persia with a six-week Esther Bible study called *Becoming Women God Could Use*. At the conclusion of this study, we celebrated with a One Night with a King.

The proceeding shut-ins included:
- 🌸 Walking Together in Prayer: Rejoice, Restoration, and Revival;
- 🌸 Judging Others;
- 🌸 Our Defining Moment;
- 🌸 Women Anointed in the Lord;
- 🌸 The Tabernacle;
- 🌸 In His Steps;
- 🌸 Weeping Women of God;
- 🌸 A Touch of Heaven in 2011;

- In the Meantime, What Are We Going to Do while We Wait for God to Move?;
- Teach Them to Weep;
- Prayer (Matthew 6:9–13);
- Make Jesus Number One (Heart, Soul, Mind, Body);
- It's Application Time!;
- Glory Overflow;
- Lioness Arising;
- Deliverance;
- Holy Is a BADD Four-Letter Word;
- Shhhhhhh and WAIT…Momentum;
- A Conversation with God;
- "What Prayer Is & What Prayer Is Not"

The essence of this collection of experiences and testimonies is to encourage you and to spark a desire or interest to pause in His presence. You don't need an agenda; you can shut in alone or with a group of sister-friends.

God is aware that many of His daughters are standing at the outer court with a desire to be that vessel in which He can dwell. Our prayer is that we 'press in' individually and collectively in our communion with the Lord. As He leads us, may His strength be the wind on our backs, catapulting us to be His light and His salt in our Jerusalem's, Judea's, Samaria's, and to the uttermost parts of the earth.

EPILOGUE

If you have never asked Jesus to be your Lord and Savior,
or if you would like to rededicate your life,
PAUSE and consider doing so today.
It's as easy as A, B, C.

ADMIT
"All have sinned and fall short of the glory of God"
(Romans 3:23).

❖❖❖❖

BELIEVE
"For God so loved the world that He gave His only begotten
Son, that whoever believes in Him should not perish
but have everlasting life"
(John 3:16).

❖❖❖❖

CALL
"Whoever calls on the name of the Lord shall be saved"
(Romans 10:13).

*If you have repeated these A, B, C's,
pick a book in the Bible and begin reading.
If you don't have a church home, locate a Bible-believing church,
and let them know the decision you have made today!*

Congratulations and welcome to the family of God.

BIBLIOGRAPHY

References

Unless otherwise indicated, all scriptures quotations are taken from King James Version/Amplified Parallel Bible, Zondervan Publishing House - 1995.

Life Application, The Living Bible Copyright ©1971. Used by permission of Tyndale House Publishers, Inc., Wheaton, Illinois 60189.

The Holy Bible, English Standard Version Copyright © 2001 by Crossway Bibles, a division of Good News Publishers.

Unless otherwise indicated, all definitions are taken from the Merriam-Webster. Merriam-Webster, n.d. Web. 03 June 2014.

Copyright © 2014, Bible Study Tools. All rights reserved. Article Images Copyright © 2014 JupiterImages Corporation.

"Bible Gateway." BibleGateway.com: A Searchable Online Bible in over 100 Versions and 50 Languages. N.p., n.d. Web. 03 June 2014.

Answers. Answers Corporation, n.d. Web. 03 June 2014.

"Wiki Answers." Wikipedia. Wikimedia Foundation, 17 May 2014. Web. 10 March 2014.

Encyclopedia Britannica Online. Encyclopedia Britannica, n.d. Web. 02 February 2014.

Lockyer, Herbert. All the Women of the Bible: The Life and times of All the Women of the Bible. Grand Rapids: Zondervan Pub. House, 1967. Print.

Spurgeon, Charles. "The Spurgeon Archive." The Spurgeon Archive. N.p., n.d. Web. 04 June 2014.Snare of the Fowler Delivered on Sabbath Morning, March 29, 1857, by then REV. C. H.

Spurgeon at the Music Hall, Royal Surrey Gardens The Spurgeon Archives.

Eddie, Brother. "Prayer Meeting Tips." JustPray.org : How to Pray
for Revival. N.p., n.d. Web. 03 June 2014.

Finney, Charles G. "Lecture VIII Meetings For Prayer." Lectures
on Revivals of Religion. New York: Leavitt, Lord, 1835. N.
pag. Print.

Murray, Andrew. "Chapter 35 Prayer-Meetings." The New Life:
Words of God for Young Disciples of Christ. New York:
Hurst, 1891. N. pag. Print.

Torrey, R. A. What the Bible Teaches: The Truths of the Bible
Made Plain, Simple and Understandable. Peabody, MA:
Hendrickson, 1998. Print.

Wilderness, The Tabernacle In The, By Keith Cook, and --
Table Of Contents --. The Tabernacle in the Wilderness
by Keith Cook -- Table of Contents -- (n.d.): n.
pag. Breadoflifebiblestudy.com. Web.

"Bible History Online Images and Resources for Biblical
History." Bible History Online Images and Resources for
Biblical History. N.p., n.d. Web. 03 June 2014.

Piper, John, and Wayne A. Grudem. Recovering Biblical Manhood
and Womanhood: A Response to Evangelical Feminism.
Wheaton, IL: Crossway, 1991. Print.

"RayStedman.org." Authentic Christianity, "Adventuring Through
the Bible." Authentic Christianity. N.p., n.d. Web. 03 June
2014.

Heald, Cynthia. Becoming a Woman of Prayer: A Bible Study.
Colorado Springs, CO: NavPress, 1996. Print.

Willmington, H. L. Willmington's Guide to the Bible. Wheaton,
IL: Tyndale House, 1981. Print.

"Tabernacle Model Kit, Tabernacle of Moses Videos and Free
Sunday School Lessons." Tabernacle Model Kit, Tabernacle
of Moses Videos and Free Sunday School Lessons. N.p.,
n.d. Web. 37 June 2014.

Chambers, Oswald. Devotions for Morning and Evening with
Oswald Chambers: The Complete Daily Devotions of My
Utmost for His Highest and Daily Thoughts for Disciples.

New York, NY: Inspirational, 1994. Print.

Madison, Randy F. Pursuing Intimacy with God: Life's #1 Priority. Waco, TX: PCG Legacy, 2010. Print.

"MEETINGS FOR PRAYER by Charles G. Finney." MEETINGS FOR PRAYER by Charles G. Finney. N.p., n.d. Web. 04 June 2014.

"An OnLine Site for the Complete WORKS of CHARLES G. FINNEY." An OnLine Site for the Complete WORKS of CHARLES G. FINNEY. N.p., n.d. Web. 07 June 2014.

"Color Symbolism and Color Meaning in The Bible." Color Symbolism in The Bible and Color Meanings. N.p., n.d. Web. 07 June 2014.

"Home Improvement Dos and Don'ts." HGTV Design Blog Design Happens. N.p., n.d. Web. 02 May 2014.

"Lighting." Design Ideas with Pictures for Living Rooms, Bathrooms, Kitchens, & More. N.p., n.d. Web. 07 June 2014.

Taylor, Somer. "How Is Gold Purified?" EHow. Demand Media, 08 Apr. 2009. Web. 06 March 2014.

Kiefer, Heather Mason, Contributing Editor. Empty Seats: Fewer Families Eat Together. Gallup Week In Review. 20 January 2004. Web.

"The Tabernacle in the Wilderness." The Tabernacle in the Wilderness. N.p., n.d. Web. 10 January 2014.

"Streams in the Desert." *Womens World Day of Prayer Welcome to Womens World Day Of Prayer Comments*. N.p., n.d. Web. 16 March 2014.

"About the Day — Pay It Forward Day." *About the Day — Pay It Forward Day*. N.p., n.d. Web. 07 June 2014.

"Brian Bill Sermon on Why We Need Each Other." *Http://www. sermoncentral.com*. N.p., n.d. Web. 07 June 2014.

"Most U.S. Families Still Routinely Dine Together at Home." *Most U.S. Families Still Routinely Dine Together at Home*. N.p., n.d. Web. 06 June 2014.

"USA Copyright Law for Musical Works." United States Copyright Law. N.p., n.d. Web. 30 Aug. 2014.

ABOUT THE AUTHOR

Sheri Powell and her husband Anthony reside in Florida. They have five adult children, one grandson, and a bouquet of family and friends.

Sheri has an extensive chronicle of volunteering and mentorship with inner-city children, youth ministry, the Boys & Girls Club, and various women's groups. Sheri lives to encourage women of all ages that every season of their life has a purpose.

Though Sheri possesses a Bachelor's in Church Ministry and an Associate of Arts in Christian Counseling, she does not let degrees or titles define her. God has given her a slideshow of her life. In it, the Spirit of the Lord God is upon her, and the LORD has anointed her to preach good tidings unto the meek. He is sending her to bind up the brokenhearted, to proclaim liberty to the captives, to open the prison to them who are bound ... and to comfort all who mourn (Isaiah 61:1-3 & Luke 4:18-19).

Sheri is also the author of another published book titled *Pausing With God: A Journey Through Menopause.* She lives and breathes to simply do God's will. With an inherent desire to Share the Lord with People, Sheri founded and created the SLP Company. Its goal is to share available resources that can help willing participants be all that God has created them to be. Sheri looks forward to watching God show up and show His creation that He is who He says He is and will do what He has said He will do.

If you have a testimony or would like to share your shut-in experience, write us at:

Sheri Powell
C/O SLP Company
P. O. Box 9172
Fleming Isle, FL 32006